MILLIONAIRE STARTING NOW

THE FAST TRACK TO SEVEN FIGURES

DESHAWN PRICE

HERITAGE
PUBLISHING

This book is dedicated to the builders — the ones who got tired of waiting, tired of wishing, and finally chose to move. To those who decided that "someday" was too expensive and "now" was the only affordable start date. To the disciplined few who are willing to trade comfort for capacity, distraction for direction, and excuses for execution.

It is for the early risers and late grinders. For the quiet planners and the relentless finishers. For those who kept working when results were invisible and kept improving when applause was absent. For every person who chose ownership over blame and action over explanation.

This is dedicated to the learners who became doers, the doers who became builders, and the builders who became multipliers.

To the risk-takers who calculated carefully and moved anyway. To the focused who said no often so they could say yes to what mattered most. To those who respected money enough to manage it and respected time enough to invest it.

And above all, this is dedicated to the version of you who refused to stay where you started.

You didn't just read about growth.

You decided to build it.

Wealth is not created by wishing more, waiting longer, or knowing everything — it is created by deciding, building, repeating, and scaling.

Small disciplined actions, executed daily and improved relentlessly, will outrun raw talent, perfect timing, and lucky breaks.

Start before you feel ready.

Measure what matters.

Multiply what works.

The first dollar proves it's possible.

The next thousand prove it's repeatable.

The first million proves it was built on purpose.

FOREWORD

There are two kinds of money books in the world. The first kind makes you feel inspired for a few hours. The second kind changes how you operate for years. The difference is not in how loudly they motivate, but in how clearly they instruct. Inspiration without execution fades. Structure with action compounds. This book was written to be the second kind.

Millionaire Starting Now — The Fast Track to Seven Figures does not treat wealth like a lottery ticket or a personality trait. It treats wealth like a buildable system. That is a critical distinction. Systems can be learned. Systems can be repeated. Systems can be improved. And systems — when executed with discipline — can be scaled. You are not being handed hype here. You are being handed a framework.

What makes this work powerful is its bias toward movement. Too many capable people stay stuck in preparation mode. They read, plan, outline, and optimize — but rarely deploy. This book confronts that stall point head-on. It replaces vague ambition with measurable behavior. It turns ideas into quotas, goals into metrics, and intention into daily operating rhythm. It insists that progress is not proven by thought, but by output.

You will notice something else as you read: the repeated return to fundamentals. Value creation. Offer strength. Skill stacking. Cash discipline. Systems leverage. These are not trendy tactics — they are durable drivers. Markets change, tools evolve, platforms rise and fall, but these principles remain profitable across cycles. Builders who master them are never starting from zero, even when they must start again.

This foreword is not written to congratulate you for buying a book. It is written to challenge you to use one. The material ahead will only reward applied readers. Margin notes will matter more than passive page turns. Implementation will matter more than agreement. Testing will matter more than theory. If you execute even a fraction of what is outlined here with consistency, your financial trajectory will change.

Do not rush this — but do not delay it either. Study with urgency. Apply with courage. Measure with honesty. Adjust with humility. Continue with discipline.

Seven figures is not built by wishing you had started earlier.

It is built by being glad you started now.

INTRODUCTION

Most people don't fail to reach seven figures because they lack intelligence, talent, or opportunity. They fail because they never truly start. They circle the runway. They over-research. They wait for perfect timing, perfect clarity, perfect confidence. Meanwhile, wealth is being built by people who simply decided to move. **This book is your line in the sand.**

Millionaire Starting Now — The Fast Track to Seven Figures is not theory. It is not motivational fluff. It is not a slow, comfortable stroll through financial ideas. It is a field manual for decisive action, income creation, and scalable execution. You are not here to be entertained — you are here to build.

Seven figures is not reserved for the lucky, the connected, or the born-privileged. It is built by operators who understand value, speed, leverage, and discipline. The modern economy rewards problem-solvers, creators, and executors at unprecedented levels. The door is not closed. It is wide open — but it does not stay open for the hesitant.

This book will challenge delay. It will confront excuse

patterns. It will replace vague goals with measurable targets and replace passive learning with immediate implementation. You will learn how to generate income quickly, convert skill into revenue, design offers that sell, and build momentum that compounds. Not someday. Not after one more course. **Now.**

You do not need a perfect background. You need a profitable direction. You do not need more motivation. You need a working model and the courage to deploy it. Progress favors motion. Revenue favors value. Scale favors structure.

Read this like a builder, not a browser. Mark it up. Apply it fast. Test aggressively. Adjust intelligently. Move relentlessly.

The starting line is not next year. Not next month. Not next Monday.

Your starting line is now.

PREFACE

This book was not written for the curious observer. It was written for the committed builder. There is a difference between someone who likes the idea of wealth and someone who is ready to construct it. One reads for interest. The other reads for instruction and immediately looks for a place to apply it. If you are holding this book, the assumption is simple: you are ready to move.

The title is intentional. *Millionaire Starting Now* is not about background, privilege, timing, or luck. It is about decision and direction. Too many capable people postpone financial progress while waiting for better conditions. Better conditions rarely arrive on schedule. Meanwhile, years pass and opportunities rotate to those already in motion. This book argues that intelligent speed beats perfect timing, and structured execution beats prolonged preparation.

You will not find fantasy formulas here. There is no secret loophole, hidden shortcut, or overnight transformation promise in these pages. Instead, you will find models, methods, and mental frameworks that convert effort into measurable economic progress. You will see repeated emphasis on value creation, disciplined action, offer strength, skill stacking, leverage, and reinvestment. These themes appear often because they work often. Repetition is not redundancy — it is reinforcement.

The chapters are designed to function like build modules. Each one strengthens a specific part of your financial engine. Decision. Income acceleration. Skills. Execution rhythm. Opportunity detection. Offer design. Leverage. Cash control. Scale discipline. Momentum. Expansion. None of these stand alone at seven figures. Together, they form a structure capable of carrying that weight. You are encouraged not just to read chapters, but to install them.

You may feel challenged at points while reading. That is deliberate. Comfort rarely produces transformation. Some sections will confront delay habits, excuse patterns, and undisciplined money behavior directly. Not to condemn — but to clear the obstruction between you and your stated goals. Pressure, when applied correctly, produces progress.

Use this book actively. Underline aggressively. Write action steps in the margins. Turn concepts into checklists. Turn checklists into calendar blocks. Turn calendar blocks into shipped work. Knowledge that is not scheduled is rarely executed. Execution is the only bridge between this preface and your first million.

You do not need to know everything before you begin.

You need to begin — and keep building.

1

DECISION DAY: DRAWING THE LINE BETWEEN WANTING WEALTH AND BUILDING IT

Decision Day is the moment where wishing ends and building begins, where desire stops being emotional and starts becoming operational. Most people say they want wealth, but very few define the exact behaviors that create it. Wanting is comfortable because it costs nothing and risks nothing. Building is uncomfortable because it demands structure, sacrifice, and sustained execution. The line between the two is not drawn with ideas but with action. You cross it when you assign deadlines to your dreams and numbers to your goals. You cross it when your calendar changes, not just your thoughts. You cross it when entertainment loses priority and production takes first place. Wealth does not respond to interest; it responds to commitment. Decision Day is where you stop negotiating with your own potential and start commanding your direction.

On Decision Day, you stop asking whether wealth is possible and start asking what must be done next. Vague intention is replaced with measurable targets and defined outputs. Instead of saying you want to be a millionaire, you define income streams, value creation paths, and production quotas. You stop consuming endless information and start converting knowledge into revenue-producing moves. You no longer admire successful people from a distance; you reverse-engineer their behaviors. The question shifts from "Can I?" to "How will I?" and then to "By when?" Clarity is created through writing, planning, and committing, not through waiting for inspiration. Momentum begins when metrics appear. Your goals must become visible, trackable, and reviewable. Decision Day turns dreams into assignments.

Many people delay their financial breakthrough because they are addicted to preparation without performance. They polish plans that are never launched and refine ideas that are never tested. They confuse motion with progress and research with results. Decision Day breaks that cycle with a bias toward controlled action. Imperfect execution beats perfect hesitation every time in the wealth-building arena. Markets reward those who show up with value, not those who hide with theories. You learn more from one live offer than from fifty private notes. Feedback from reality is more valuable than approval from imagination. When you decide, you enter the arena of evidence. Builders get data, and data creates improvement.

Drawing the line between wanting and building requires identity change before income change. You must stop seeing yourself as someone trying to make money and start seeing yourself as someone who produces value at scale. Identity drives behavior, and behavior drives outcomes. If you still think like a dabbler, you will act like a dabbler. If you think like an operator, you will schedule, measure, and ship like one. Decision Day is an identity declaration backed by behavioral proof. You set non-negotiable work blocks and protect them like assets. You create output quotas that must be met regardless of mood. You measure days by production, not by activity. You become accountable to results, not effort alone.

Real wealth building is less about intensity spikes and more about structured consistency. Decision Day installs systems where emotions used to rule. Instead of working when you feel motivated, you work when it is scheduled. Instead of guessing priorities, you execute predefined revenue tasks first. Discipline becomes automated through design. Checklists replace guesswork and dashboards replace denial. You track leads, offers, conversions, and output volume. You make your progress visible so your excuses become obvious. Structure removes drama and increases speed. Consistency compounds faster than brilliance. The builder wins because the builder repeats.

Decision Day also eliminates financial fantasy thinking and replaces it with value economics. Money flows toward solved problems and delivered outcomes. You stop asking how to get paid and start asking what results you can create. Income becomes a scoreboard of usefulness, not luck. You train yourself to see every skill as a potential revenue tool. You develop the habit of packaging, pricing, and presenting value. You learn to attach numbers to benefits and timelines to delivery. The marketplace is not mysterious when you think in outcomes. People pay for transformation, relief, speed, and advantage. Builders study demand and answer it directly.

Risk looks different after Decision Day because you redefine what is truly dangerous. It is more dangerous to drift for years than to test for months. It is more dangerous to delay skill development than to endure early mistakes. It is more dangerous to stay invisible than to launch imperfectly. Action contains risk, but stagnation guarantees loss. Builders take intelligent, bounded risks with measured downside and meaningful upside. You test small, learn fast, and scale what works. You stop betting your future on comfort. You start investing your effort into capability. Fear becomes a signal to prepare, not a command to retreat. Courage becomes scheduled behavior, not a rare emotion.

Decision Day forces you to confront distraction as an income killer. Every hour has an economic direction whether you admit it or not. Time either compounds assets or compounds regret. Builders assign roles to hours before hours disappear. You reduce low-value consumption and increase high-value creation. You design your environment to make productive work easier to start. Friction is removed from revenue tasks and added to distraction habits. Notifications lose power over your schedule. Focus becomes a financial strategy, not just a productivity trick. Deep work becomes a daily requirement. Attention becomes your most guarded investment.

Commitment becomes real when you build consequence into your plan. Decision Day is strengthened when failure to act has a cost. You create public targets, partner accountability, or financial stakes. You report progress weekly and adjust visibly. Measurement replaces mood as the judge of effort. You stop letting yourself disappear into private delay. Transparency increases follow-through. Review sessions replace vague self-reflection. You treat your goals like contracts, not preferences. Standards become enforceable. Progress becomes undeniable.

Decision Day is not loud, flashy, or dramatic, but it is irreversible when done correctly. It is a quiet internal contract backed by daily external proof. From that day forward, you stop browsing opportunity and start building engines. You stop collecting ideas and start deploying assets. You stop admiring results and start manufacturing them. The gap between wanting and building closes through repeated execution. Seven figures is not reached by a single leap but by thousands of kept decisions. Each kept decision is a brick, and each brick is placed on purpose. You are not waiting anymore. You are constructing now. The fast track begins the moment the decision becomes behavior.

2

THE INCOME ACCELERATION BLUEPRINT: HOW TO CREATE CASH FLOW FAST

The Income Acceleration Blueprint begins with a simple truth most people avoid: speed matters when building wealth. Slow improvement is admirable, but fast cash flow changes your options, your confidence, and your leverage. You cannot scale what you cannot first fund. Early cash flow is the oxygen of your seven-figure engine. Without it, ideas suffocate and plans stall. With it, experiments multiply and opportunities expand. Acceleration is not recklessness; it is focused velocity applied to value creation. The goal is not frantic motion but directed output. You are not chasing money; you are engineering inflow. Fast cash flow is built, not found.

Cash flow grows fastest when you stop trying to be impressive and start trying to be useful. The market pays for solved problems, not personal passion alone. Income acceleration comes from identifying urgent needs and delivering practical solutions. You look for pain points, bottlenecks, delays, and confusions that people will gladly pay to remove. You choose problems that are expensive to ignore. You design offers that reduce time, increase revenue, or remove frustration. You speak in outcomes, not features. You price based on value delivered, not hours spent. Utility beats elegance in the early stages. Fast money follows functional help.

The blueprint demands that you prioritize high-income skills over low-income busywork. Not all effort pays equally, and pretending otherwise is financially dangerous. High-income skills connect directly to revenue generation, cost reduction, or growth. Examples include sales, copywriting, offer creation, lead generation, and process optimization. These skills move money, not just information. You can learn them faster than you think through focused practice and real projects. You do not need mastery to start; you need capability to deliver. Skill acquisition becomes tied to immediate application. Learning without earning is minimized. Practice happens in the marketplace, not just in notebooks.

Income acceleration also requires ruthless clarity about your current asset base. You inventory your skills, network, tools, knowledge, and access. Hidden earning power often sits unused because it feels ordinary to you. What is easy for you may be valuable to others. You translate your abilities into services, products, or packaged outcomes. You stop asking what job you can get and start asking what result you can sell. You bundle what you know into clear solutions. Packaging increases perceived value and speeds buying decisions. Clarity converts capability into cash. Vagueness delays income.

Speed comes from shortening the distance between offer creation and offer presentation. Many people build endlessly before showing anyone anything. The blueprint flips that pattern and moves presentation earlier. You create minimum viable offers and bring them to real buyers fast. Early offers are simple, outcome-focused, and clearly priced. Feedback is gathered through transactions, not opinions. Buyers teach you how to improve faster than observers. Revenue becomes research. Each sale funds refinement. Each conversation sharpens positioning. You iterate in public with purpose. Speed of exposure increases speed of income.

Direct outreach is one of the most underrated income accelerators available. Waiting to be discovered is slow and unreliable. Builders initiate conversations with potential buyers, partners, and clients. You send proposals, messages, and targeted pitches daily. Volume plus relevance produces opportunity. You learn to communicate value clearly and briefly. Rejection becomes data, not defeat. Response rates become metrics you improve. Outreach becomes scheduled, not emotional. Conversations create conversions. Silence is replaced with pipeline.

The blueprint insists on stacking income streams instead of babysitting one fragile source. Early diversification reduces risk and increases velocity. You combine active income with semi-leveraged income where possible. Services, digital products, commissions, and performance deals can coexist. Each stream feeds the others through cross-promotion and shared audiences. You do not wait for one stream to perfect before adding another. You build in layers with managed complexity. Multiple streams create stability and acceleration. Cash flow becomes less brittle. Redundancy increases resilience.

Pricing strategy plays a critical role in how fast cash arrives. Underpricing slows growth and overloads your capacity. The blueprint teaches value-based pricing instead of fear-based pricing. You charge in proportion to outcomes, not effort alone. Higher prices allow reinvestment in tools, talent, and reach. Serious buyers often respect premium positioning more than bargain offers. You justify price with clarity, proof, and guarantees where appropriate. Margin fuels momentum. Cheap work creates exhaustion. Strong pricing creates expansion. Revenue per transaction matters.

Income acceleration is amplified through partnerships and proximity. Working with people who already have customers is faster than finding customers alone. You seek collaborations where your skill solves their bottleneck. Revenue-sharing deals can open doors faster than fixed fees. You plug into existing distribution channels. Trust transfers through association. You become a value-adding extension, not a random vendor. Strategic alliances compress timelines. Warm audiences convert faster than cold markets. Shared wins build lasting networks. Proximity multiplies pace.

The Income Acceleration Blueprint only works when tracked with visible metrics and weekly reviews. You measure offers made, conversations started, deals closed, and cash collected. Numbers remove illusion and guide adjustment. Weekly review turns activity into strategy. You double down on what pays and delete what delays. Speed improves when feedback loops tighten. You become a student of your own scoreboard. Progress becomes engineered, not guessed. Cash flow becomes predictable through pattern recognition. Acceleration becomes repeatable through measurement. Fast income stops being luck and starts being design.

3

SKILL STACKS THAT PAY: TURNING ABILITY INTO HIGH-VALUE EARNINGS

Skill stacks that pay are not built by accident, and they are not built by talent alone. They are deliberately assembled combinations of abilities that multiply earning power. A single skill can earn income, but a stack of complementary skills can command premium value. The marketplace rewards people who can connect multiple functions into one outcome. When you combine persuasion with technical ability, or strategy with execution, you become harder to replace. High earners are rarely one-dimensional operators. They are translators between problems and solutions across domains. Each added skill increases your range and your rate. Skill stacking is economic compounding in human form. Your goal is not to be interesting, but indispensable.

Most people approach learning like collectors instead of builders. They gather random knowledge without economic direction. A paying skill stack is designed backward from market demand. You start with outcomes people already spend money to achieve. Then you identify the skill layers required to produce those outcomes reliably. You do not chase trendy skills; you chase profitable intersections. Each skill is selected because it strengthens the others. The stack is coherent, not scattered. Learning becomes strategic instead of recreational. Direction replaces distraction. The result is capability that converts.

A powerful starter stack for high-value earnings often includes communication, persuasion, and problem diagnosis. If you can understand a problem, explain a solution, and motivate action, you can generate revenue. Communication turns complexity into clarity. Persuasion turns interest into decision. Diagnosis turns symptoms into root-cause solutions. Together, these three dramatically increase your economic usefulness. They apply across industries and platforms. They improve every offer you present. They increase conversion in every conversation. They are force multipliers for nearly every other skill. This is why they belong in your early stack.

Technical skills gain economic power when paired with commercial skills. Coding plus sales beats coding alone. Design plus copy beats design alone. Data plus storytelling beats data alone. The builder mindset asks, "What second skill makes this first skill more valuable?" Pairing creation with distribution is especially profitable. Many creators struggle because they cannot market their output. When you can both build and sell, you control the full value chain. Dependence decreases and margins increase. You stop waiting for opportunity and start generating it. Combination creates command.

Skill stacks that pay are built through applied projects, not passive study. Reading about a skill does not stack it; using it does. Real projects force integration across abilities. Deadlines create pressure that accelerates learning. Client work exposes gaps faster than courses. Each project becomes a laboratory for stacking. Reflection after execution turns experience into insight. You document what worked and what failed. You refine process with each repetition. Your stack becomes sharper through use. Applied learning locks skills together.

The speed of your earning growth depends on how fast you close your skill gaps. Avoiding weak areas delays income expansion. Builders identify their bottlenecks and attack them directly. If you cannot sell, you train selling. If you cannot present, you practice presenting. If you cannot negotiate, you study negotiation. Weak links limit strong chains. Courage in skill development produces financial lift. You turn embarrassment into education. You schedule practice like production. Improvement becomes intentional. Gaps become targets, not secrets.

High-value skill stacks also include leverage skills that extend your output. Automation, delegation, and system design belong in your stack. These skills allow your work to travel farther without your constant presence. You learn to document processes so others can execute them. You design workflows that reduce repeated effort. You use tools that multiply reach and speed. Leverage turns labor into scale. Scale turns effort into wealth potential. Without leverage skills, income stays capped by hours. With them, output detaches from time. That is where seven-figure paths open.

Positioning is a skill that dramatically increases the pay of your stack. Two people with identical abilities can earn vastly different amounts based on positioning. Specialists who solve costly problems earn more than generalists who do many small tasks. You learn to describe your stack in outcome language. You claim a problem domain instead of a task list. You build proof through case results and clear messaging. You align your stack with a defined buyer group.

Relevance increases response. Clarity increases price tolerance. Positioning turns skill into brand. Brand turns skill into premium demand.

Skill stacks must be refreshed and extended as markets evolve. What pays today may pay less tomorrow. Builders schedule skill upgrades as a career discipline. You monitor trends in demand and tools. You add adjacent skills before old ones decline. Adaptation protects income velocity. Curiosity becomes a financial asset. Stagnation becomes a warning sign. You run quarterly skill audits on yourself. You ask what to add, what to deepen, and what to drop. Your stack remains alive and aligned. Evolution sustains earnings.

Turning ability into high-value earnings is ultimately about intentional design and relentless application. You are not waiting to be discovered; you are engineering usefulness. Each skill you add must earn its place through market relevance. Each layer must increase your problem-solving power. You practice until integration feels natural. You measure results, not just learning hours. You present your stack through offers, not resumes. You refine through feedback and revenue signals. Over time, your stack becomes your signature advantage. Income follows integrated capability. Skill stacks that pay are built by builders who never stop stacking.

4

EXECUTION OVER EXCUSES: THE MILLIONAIRE WORK RHYTHM

Execution over excuses is the dividing line between financial aspiration and financial arrival. Many people sincerely desire success, but sincerity without sustained execution produces nothing measurable. The marketplace does not reward intention; it rewards completed value. Millionaire builders operate on a work rhythm that converts plans into shipped outcomes. They treat action as a daily obligation, not a conditional reaction. Excuses are recognized as emotional substitutes for discipline. Every excuse feels reasonable in the moment and expensive in the long run. Execution feels demanding in the moment and profitable in the long run. The millionaire work rhythm is not about intensity bursts but repeatable output cycles. It is structured, scheduled, and defended. Results grow where execution repeats.

The first principle of the millionaire work rhythm is that production comes before preference. You do the work that moves revenue before the work that feels comfortable. Priority is determined by economic impact, not emotional ease. High-value tasks are placed at the front of the day.

Energy is invested where returns are highest. Builders do not ask what they feel like doing; they ask what moves the metric. This removes daily negotiation with mood. Discipline becomes pre-decided through planning. Important work is started before distractions wake up. Preference follows progress, not the other way around.

Execution becomes reliable when work is converted into defined blocks instead of vague intentions. Time blocks create containers for output. You assign specific revenue-driving tasks to specific hours. This transforms work from optional to scheduled. What is scheduled gets done more often than what is merely desired. The clock becomes an accountability partner. You protect these blocks from interruption like financial assets. You measure block completion rates weekly. You adjust duration based on performance data. Structure removes ambiguity from effort. Predictable structure produces predictable progress.

The millionaire work rhythm is built on daily minimum outputs that must be met regardless of circumstances. Output quotas replace open-ended effort. You define non-negotiable deliverables for each day. These may include offers sent, pages written, calls made, or campaigns launched. Minimums create momentum even on low-energy days. Small completions prevent total stall. Consistency beats sporadic brilliance in wealth creation. Quotas turn work into a scoreboard. Scoreboards drive behavior improvement. Behavior improvement drives income growth. Minimums make progress durable.

Excuses lose power when they are named, tracked, and confronted directly. Most excuses repeat in predictable patterns. You write them down when they appear. You study their triggers and timing. Awareness reduces their control. You build counter-responses in advance. If distraction appears, a preplanned fallback task begins. If energy drops, a shorter high-value task is triggered. You replace excuse pathways with action pathways. You make it easier to continue than to quit. Friction is placed in the path of avoidance. Awareness turns excuses into signals for adjustment.

The millionaire work rhythm depends on rapid start behavior. Delay at the beginning of a task is one of the greatest productivity leaks. Builders train themselves to begin before they feel ready. Starting creates clarity faster than thinking. Action generates energy that hesitation never will. You use countdown starts and environment cues. You remove setup barriers ahead of time. Tools are prepared before the block begins. First steps are defined in writing. Entry becomes automatic. Fast starts multiply finished work. Finished work multiplies results.

Recovery is built into the rhythm so execution remains sustainable. Exhaustion destroys consistency if unmanaged. Millionaire builders plan renewal as seriously as production. Breaks are scheduled, not stolen. Sleep is treated as performance fuel. Exercise supports cognitive endurance. Nutrition stabilizes energy output. Renewal protects decision quality. Decision quality protects income direction. Sustainable pace beats heroic burnout. Recovery is a strategic advantage. Endurance outperforms spurts.

Measurement is the metronome of the millionaire work rhythm. What gets measured gets improved. You track execution metrics daily and review them weekly. Metrics include hours of deep work, outputs completed, and revenue actions taken. Data replaces self-deception. Patterns become visible quickly. Weak days are corrected faster. Strong days are analyzed and replicated. Measurement creates feedback loops. Feedback loops accelerate refinement. Refinement accelerates earnings. The rhythm tightens with tracking.

Environment design supports execution more than motivation ever will. You shape your workspace for focus and flow. Distractions are removed or blocked. Tools are within reach and ready. Visual cues remind you of targets and metrics. Default settings favor production. Digital noise is minimized. Friction is reduced for high-value tasks. Convenience is reduced for low-value habits. Your environment votes for your success daily. Surroundings become silent partners in execution.

Execution over excuses ultimately becomes identity, not just behavior. You stop seeing yourself as someone trying to be disciplined. You see yourself as someone who executes regardless of mood. Identity-level commitment stabilizes performance. The millionaire work rhythm becomes your normal pattern. Action becomes your default response. Output becomes your daily language. Results become your predictable byproduct. Excuses lose their voice when execution gains authority. Rhythm replaces randomness. Builders are built by their routines. Seven figures are reached by those who execute when others explain.

5

OPPORTUNITY MINING: FINDING PROFITABLE GAPS OTHERS IGNORE

Opportunity mining is the disciplined practice of searching for profit where others see inconvenience, confusion, or complexity. Most people look where the spotlight is brightest, but builders search where the need is strongest. The loudest markets are often the most crowded. The quieter corners often contain unmet demand and underpriced value. Millionaire builders develop the habit of scanning for friction. Wherever people complain, delay, overpay, or struggle, a gap is forming. Gaps are invitations for value creation. Value creation is the root of revenue acceleration. You are not hunting trends; you are detecting inefficiencies. Opportunity mining turns irritation into income. The ignored becomes profitable in trained hands.

Profitable gaps often hide behind repeated customer frustration. When people say, "Why is this so hard?" they are revealing a business opening. Complaints are unpolished market research. Builders collect them instead of dismissing them. You listen in reviews, forums, support threads, and conversations. Patterns matter more than volume. Repeated friction signals real demand. Demand plus dissatisfaction equals opportunity space. You document these signals instead of scrolling past them. You translate frustration into solution concepts. You rank problems by urgency and willingness to pay. The louder the pain, the faster the purchase.

Opportunity mining requires learning to see processes instead of products. Most people see the finished item, but builders see the broken steps behind it. Every multi-step process contains drop-off points and delays. Each drop-off is a potential intervention point. Simplifying a step can be more profitable than reinventing the whole system. You map workflows in industries you study. You ask where time, money, or accuracy is lost. Small efficiency gains can command large fees. Optimization is often more valuable than invention. Builders improve pipelines, not just outputs. Process vision reveals hidden profit. Systems thinking uncovers silent gaps.

Ignored customer segments frequently contain high-yield opportunity. Many markets overlook smaller or specialized groups. Builders ask who is underserved, not just who is numerous. Niche groups often have urgent needs and fewer tailored solutions. Specificity increases conversion and loyalty. You study subgroups inside larger categories. You identify language, constraints, and priorities unique to them. Tailored solutions outperform generic ones. Specialization reduces competition. Relevance increases pricing power. Small audiences can produce large income. Neglected segments reward focused builders.

Geographic and logistical gaps also produce overlooked profit channels. Not every region receives equal service quality or speed. Distribution inefficiencies create opportunity windows. Builders notice where delivery is slow or options are limited. Localizing solutions can outperform global generalists. You look for distance between supply and demand. Bridging that distance creates value. Access itself can be monetized. Convenience is a premium feature. Speed is a competitive edge. Logistics is often a hidden goldmine. Movement creates margin.

Information gaps are among the most profitable and fastest to fill. When people lack clarity, they seek guidance. Confusion delays decisions and increases stress. Builders package clarity into paid solutions. Education, templates, checklists, and guided systems close knowledge gaps. You convert expertise into structured help. Step-by-step frameworks sell because they reduce uncertainty. Simplicity is marketable. Organized knowledge beats scattered facts. Instruction becomes product. Guidance becomes revenue. Clarity converts quickly.

Tool friction reveals another class of profitable gaps. When tools are powerful but difficult, opportunity exists. Builders create wrappers, tutorials, integrations, and shortcuts. You do not need to build the core technology to profit from it. You can make it easier to use. Ease increases adoption. Adoption increases demand. Demand increases revenue pathways. User experience improvements are monetizable. Support layers can be productized. Complexity is a doorway for simplifiers. Simplifiers get paid.

Opportunity mining improves when you combine cross-industry awareness. Innovations in one field often lag in another. Builders transfer proven models across sectors. What works in software may work in education. What works in retail may work in services. You study patterns, not just markets. Pattern recognition accelerates idea generation. Borrowed models reduce risk. Adaptation beats invention cost. You remix instead of starting from zero. Cross-pollination produces fresh advantage. Familiar tools in new places create profit. Insight travels well.

Validation is the filter that turns opportunity guesses into opportunity assets. Not every gap is profitable. Builders test interest before building fully. You run small offers, preorders, or pilot programs. You measure response, not applause. Real demand shows up in commitments. Early buyers are proof signals. Signals guide scaling decisions. Testing reduces waste. Evidence replaces assumption. Market response becomes your compass. Validated gaps deserve expansion.

Opportunity mining becomes a habit that compounds over time. You train yourself to ask opportunity questions daily. Where is there waste, delay, confusion, or exclusion? Who is being overlooked or underserved? What is harder than it should be? Each question sharpens your detection ability. Your awareness becomes an income engine. You stop waiting for ideas and start extracting them. Gaps become visible everywhere. Value creation becomes continuous. Continuous value creation produces continuous opportunity. Builders who mine relentlessly rarely run out of profitable ground.

6

SPEED TO MARKET: LAUNCH BEFORE YOU FEEL READY

Speed to market is the unfair advantage most aspiring millionaires delay themselves out of using. The marketplace does not reward the most polished idea first; it rewards the first useful solution delivered. Waiting until you feel fully ready is one of the most expensive emotional habits in business. Readiness is rarely a feeling that arrives before action. Confidence is usually manufactured by movement, not meditation. Builders launch while learning and refine while earning. Motion creates feedback, and feedback creates precision. The longer you wait, the more invisible you remain. Invisible offers never produce income. Speed to market converts potential into proof. Proof is what buyers trust.

Perfectionism is often procrastination wearing a professional costume. It sounds responsible, but it behaves like fear. You tell yourself you are improving the product when you are actually avoiding exposure. Exposure invites judgment, and judgment feels risky. Yet judgment is also where insight lives. Early versions teach lessons final versions never could. Imperfect launches produce real data. Real data beats imagined improvements. Builders prefer iteration over isolation. They would rather adjust in public than stall in private. Progress prefers participation.

Launching early forces clarity faster than endless planning ever will. When you must present an offer, you must define it. Definition sharpens value and removes fluff. You learn to state outcomes in simple language. You learn what matters to buyers and what does not. Market response edits your message quickly. Confusion is revealed through silence. Interest is revealed through questions. Objections reveal missing elements. Each response is instruction. Instruction accelerates refinement. Refinement accelerates revenue.

Speed to market works best when you design minimum viable offers. A minimum viable offer solves one clear problem for one clear group. It does not try to do everything. Narrow scope increases launch speed. Focus reduces build time. Early wins build confidence and capital. Capital funds improvement. Improvement expands scope. You earn the right to grow features through early delivery. Starting small is not thinking small. It is building smart. Precision beats breadth at launch.

Fear of embarrassment delays more launches than lack of skill. You imagine worst-case reactions and pause progress. Builders normalize awkward beginnings. First versions are allowed to be rough. Rough is temporary; hidden is permanent. Public attempts build courage muscles. Courage reduces delay next time. Each launch makes the next easier. Exposure becomes familiar. Familiar reduces fear. Reduced fear increases speed. Speed increases opportunity capture.

Competitive advantage often goes to the fast learner, not the early expert. Launching early puts you in learning mode with real stakes. Stakes increase attention and retention. You learn faster when outcomes matter. Buyer behavior teaches more than theory. Usage patterns reveal priorities. Support questions reveal confusion points. Refunds reveal expectation gaps. Testimonials reveal value drivers. This intelligence arrives only after launch. Fast learners overtake slow planners. Market classrooms reward attendance.

Revenue timing matters more than most beginners realize. Early cash flow changes your strategic options. It allows reinvestment in tools, talent, and traffic. Waiting delays funding and slows growth. Even small early revenue validates direction. Validation increases commitment. Commitment increases output. Output increases quality. Quality increases conversion. Conversion increases scale. Launch speed compresses the revenue timeline. Compressed timelines compound advantage.

Launching before you feel ready requires pre-decided launch triggers. Builders do not wait for emotional certainty. They set objective readiness criteria. When criteria are met, launch happens. This removes emotional veto power. Criteria may include function complete, outcome clear, and payment method active. Checklists replace hesitation. Decisions become mechanical instead of emotional. Mechanical decisions happen faster. Faster decisions produce earlier exposure. Earlier exposure produces earlier data. Data produces better decisions.

Speed to market improves when you separate version one from version forever. Version one is for learning, not legacy. You give yourself permission to improve publicly. Buyers respect responsiveness more than flawlessness. Updates signal commitment. Progress signals professionalism. Transparency builds trust. Iteration builds quality. Quality builds reputation. Reputation builds demand.

Demand builds revenue. Launching starts the upgrade cycle.

Launch before you feel ready is not reckless when paired with responsibility. You still deliver real value and honest promises. You still support buyers and fix faults. Speed does not remove integrity; it requires it. Builders move fast and respond faster. Accountability protects reputation. Reputation protects growth. Growth protects longevity. The window of opportunity rarely waits for comfort. Those who enter early learn early. Those who learn early earn early. Speed to market turns hesitation into head start.

7

OFFER ENGINEERING: CREATING PRODUCTS PEOPLE INSTANTLY SAY YES TO

Offer engineering is the disciplined art of designing value so clearly and compellingly that the right buyer feels immediate alignment. Most people try to sell products, but high earners build offers. A product is what it is, but an offer is how it is framed, packaged, and positioned. Millionaire builders understand that presentation multiplies perceived value. Buyers do not purchase components; they purchase outcomes and confidence. A strong offer reduces doubt and increases desire at the same time. It answers the buyer's silent questions before they are asked. It makes the next step feel obvious instead of risky. Offer engineering turns interest into action. Action is where revenue begins.

Every irresistible offer starts with a sharply defined problem and a narrowly defined buyer. General solutions for everyone convert poorly. Specific solutions for someone convert powerfully. You must know exactly who the offer is for and what pain it removes. Vague targeting produces weak messaging. Precise targeting produces magnetic language. The buyer should feel seen, not sorted. You describe their situation better than they can. That recognition builds trust quickly. Trust accelerates decision speed. Decision speed accelerates cash flow. Precision is profitable.

Outcome clarity is the core load-bearing beam of offer strength. Buyers say yes faster when the result is concrete and measurable. You do not sell features; you sell finished states. Instead of describing what the product contains, you describe what the buyer becomes. Transformation language outperforms technical language. Before-and-after contrast sharpens desire. Specific results beat abstract benefits. Numbers increase believability. Timelines increase urgency. Proof increases confidence. Clear outcomes reduce hesitation. Reduced hesitation increases conversion.

Value stacking is how elite offers feel larger than their price. You assemble multiple relevant benefits into one cohesive package. Each element supports the same core outcome. Tools, templates, support, and shortcuts can be layered together. The stack must feel unified, not random. Relevance matters more than quantity. Each added element should remove friction or increase speed. Buyers compare total solution value against price. When value visibly exceeds price, yes becomes easier. Overdelivery builds loyalty. Stacked value strengthens decisions.

Risk reversal is one of the most powerful levers in offer engineering. Buyers hesitate when they fear loss more than they desire gain. A well-designed guarantee reduces that fear. Guarantees signal confidence in your solution. Confidence transfers trust. Trust reduces friction. Conditional guarantees can protect both sides. Clear terms prevent abuse and confusion. Risk reversal increases trial willingness. Trial willingness increases conversions. Conversions increase revenue velocity. Safety accelerates sales.

Offer framing determines how the same product is

perceived and received. Price alone does not define expensive or affordable; context does. When positioned against costly alternatives, your offer gains attractiveness. When shown beside the cost of inaction, your price feels smaller. Anchoring changes perception. Comparison clarifies value. Sequencing information shapes interpretation. Builders control the frame, not just the facts. They lead the buyer through structured understanding. Understanding builds justification. Justification supports commitment. Framing directs decisions.

Urgency and scarcity, when used honestly, increase decision speed dramatically. Delay is the enemy of conversion. A reason to act now prevents endless postponement. Limited seats, timed bonuses, or capacity caps can be real constraints. Real constraints create real urgency. False urgency destroys trust, so integrity is non-negotiable. Deadlines focus attention. Focus increases action. Action increases sales. Sales increase momentum. Momentum increases scale.

Proof elements transform claims into credible promises. Testimonials, case results, demonstrations, and data reduce skepticism. Buyers trust evidence more than enthusiasm. Specific proof beats generic praise. Numbers beat adjectives. Stories beat slogans. Before-and-after evidence beats description. Screenshots, samples, and walkthroughs increase certainty. Certainty accelerates commitment. Commitment increases revenue reliability. Proof shortens the trust gap.

Simplicity in the buying decision is essential to instant yes behavior. Complex offers slow the mind and stall the sale. You remove unnecessary choices and confusing options. Clear steps replace tangled explanations. Clean pricing replaces hidden fees. Straight paths outperform branching mazes. Cognitive ease increases completion rates. The buyer should know exactly what to do next. Frictionless checkout supports impulse alignment. Simplicity converts attention into action. Easy decisions happen faster.

Offer engineering is never finished because markets and buyers evolve. You continuously test headlines, bundles, guarantees, and price points. Small tweaks can produce large conversion lifts. Builders treat offers like performance systems, not static pages. Metrics guide refinement. Feedback guides upgrades. Conversion rates reveal truth. Truth guides iteration. Iteration increases strength. Stronger offers produce faster yes decisions. Faster yes decisions build seven-figure engines.

8

THE LEVERAGE LADDER: USING SYSTEMS, ASSETS, AND PEOPLE TO MULTIPLY OUTPUT

The Leverage Ladder is the structure that turns hard work into multiplied results instead of repeated effort. Most people try to earn more by working longer, but millionaires earn more by multiplying output. Time alone does not scale, but leverage does. Leverage is the force that allows one unit of effort to produce many units of return. It is built through systems, assets, and people working in coordinated motion. Without leverage, income is capped by hours and energy. With leverage, output detaches from constant personal labor. Builders climb from manual production to multiplied production step by step. Each rung reduces strain and increases reach. The ladder is not optional for seven figures; it is essential.

The first rung of leverage is personal systems that stabilize and repeat your best work. A system is a defined, repeatable method for producing a result. When you document how you succeed, you can repeat it faster. Checklists replace memory and reduce mistakes. Templates replace reinvention and increase speed. Workflows replace guesswork and increase consistency. Systems convert talent into process.

Process creates predictability. Predictability creates scalability. Scalability creates growth capacity. You cannot multiply chaos, but you can multiply order.

Systems leverage begins with capturing your current best practices in writing. Every repeated task should be documented step by step. Documentation turns invisible skill into transferable instruction. Transferable instruction enables delegation later. You record tools used, sequences followed, and standards met. Clarity removes dependence on mood or memory. Written process reduces training time. Reduced training time increases team speed. Speed increases output volume. Volume increases revenue potential. Documentation is the seed of multiplication.

The second rung of the leverage ladder is asset creation that keeps working after you stop. Assets produce value repeatedly without repeated full effort. Digital products, intellectual property, content libraries, and automated funnels are examples. Assets are built once and deployed many times. They turn time into inventory. Inventory can be sold repeatedly. Repetition without rebuild creates margin. Margin creates reinvestment power. Asset builders escape the earn-and-reset cycle. Each asset becomes a worker on your behalf. Ownership multiplies output.

Asset leverage increases when distribution is designed alongside creation. Many creators build but never deploy effectively. A silent asset produces nothing. Builders engineer pathways for assets to reach buyers automatically. Email sequences, platforms, and partner channels extend reach. Distribution is a force multiplier. Reach multiplies return on creation time. Return funds further asset building. Asset networks become income ecosystems. Ecosystems are more stable than single streams. Stability supports scale. Scale supports seven-figure trajectories.

The third rung of the leverage ladder is tool leverage through automation and technology. Tools compress time and expand capacity. Automation handles repeatable actions without fatigue. Software executes tasks at machine speed. Builders identify repetitive actions and automate them early. Each automation frees human focus for higher-value work. Focus applied to strategy multiplies results. Tool stacks create operational lift. Lift increases throughput. Throughput increases opportunity capture. Smart tools are silent employees.

The fourth rung is people leverage, where output multiplies through coordinated human effort. Delegation is not loss of control; it is expansion of capacity. Builders assign tasks by skill alignment. Right people in right roles increase quality and speed. Clear instructions reduce error rates. Defined outcomes reduce confusion. Feedback loops improve performance. Teams produce more than individuals alone. Collaboration creates creative advantage. Shared effort multiplies reach. People leverage is a growth accelerator.

People leverage only works when leadership systems support it. Direction must be clear and measurable. Expectations must be written and visible. Accountability must be fair and consistent. Builders create scoreboards for teams, not just individuals. Scoreboards align effort with outcomes. Communication rhythms maintain momentum. Weekly reviews drive correction. Correction drives improvement. Improvement drives output. Output drives revenue. Leadership is leverage management.

Financial leverage is another rung that must be approached with discipline. Capital can multiply opportunity when used wisely. Investment in proven systems and assets accelerates growth. Borrowed resources must produce more than they cost. Builders use financial leverage for expansion, not lifestyle inflation. Return on investment becomes the guiding metric. Measured risk replaces emotional spending. Capital is assigned to multiplication engines. Engines produce returns. Returns repay capital. Financial leverage amplifies momentum. Discipline keeps it safe.

The Leverage Ladder works only when climbed intentionally and reviewed regularly. Each rung should be strengthened before the next is loaded heavily. Weak systems break under scale. Strong systems support expansion. Builders audit leverage quarterly. They ask what can be automated, documented, assetized, or delegated. Each conversion increases multiplier effect. Multipliers turn effort into enterprise. Enterprise turns income into scale. Scale turns progress into acceleration. Acceleration turns builders into millionaires. Leverage is how output grows beyond effort.

9

CASH DISCIPLINE: CONTROLLING MONEY LIKE A BUILDER, NOT A SPENDER

Cash discipline is the dividing line between people who touch money and people who multiply it. Many earn well but remain financially fragile because they manage money like consumers instead of builders. Builders treat every dollar as a worker, not a toy. Money is not just for comfort; it is for construction. When cash enters a builder's hands, it is assigned a mission. That mission is growth, stability, or multiplication. Undirected money disappears, but directed money compounds. Seven figures are rarely built by income alone; they are built by disciplined allocation. Control precedes expansion. Stewardship precedes scale. Cash discipline is the operating system of wealth.

A builder's first rule is that revenue is not profit and profit is not free cash. Confusion between these three destroys momentum. Revenue is total inflow, profit is what remains after costs, and free cash is what can be redeployed. Each layer must be measured separately. Builders read their numbers weekly, not yearly. Visibility prevents self-deception. Self-deception causes overspending. Overspending slows growth. Clean books create clean decisions. Clean decisions preserve capital. Preserved capital funds opportunity. Precision protects progress.

Cash discipline begins with pre-allocation instead of leftover allocation. Spenders use what remains after impulse. Builders decide destinations before dollars arrive. Percentages are assigned to operations, reinvestment, reserves, and personal pay. This turns money into a plan instead of a reaction. Plans reduce emotional spending. Emotional spending erodes scale. Allocation creates intentional flow. Intentional flow creates compounding structure. Structure stabilizes growth. Stability enables expansion. Pre-decision removes pressure at the moment of choice.

Builders separate operating money from personal lifestyle money early. Blending the two creates distortion and risk. When business cash feels like personal cash, discipline collapses. Separation creates clarity and control. Separate accounts enforce behavioral boundaries. Boundaries protect reinvestment capacity. Reinvestment fuels acceleration. Acceleration builds scale. Scale increases optionality. Optionality increases resilience. Financial walls create strategic freedom. Structure prevents leakage.

Expense evaluation becomes ruthless under builder discipline. Every cost must justify its existence through return or necessity. Builders ask what each dollar produces, not just what it purchases. Vanity expenses are delayed until asset engines are strong. Tools must increase speed, quality, or reach. Subscriptions are audited regularly. Waste is identified and removed. Savings are redirected into growth drivers. Efficiency increases margin. Margin increases reinvestment. Reinvestment increases velocity. Discipline turns trimming into thrust.

Reinvestment is the heartbeat of builder-style money

control. Instead of extracting maximum lifestyle early, builders feed their engines first. A defined reinvestment percentage is protected aggressively. That capital funds marketing, tools, talent, and assets. Each reinvestment cycle increases capacity. Capacity increases output. Output increases revenue. Revenue increases reinvestment size. This loop compounds powerfully over time. Early restraint creates later abundance. Delayed gratification becomes strategic leverage. Feeding the engine precedes enjoying the ride.

Builders maintain liquidity buffers because opportunity favors the prepared. Cash reserves are not laziness; they are launch fuel. Without reserves, good opportunities become stressful risks. With reserves, they become strategic moves. Liquidity reduces desperation decisions. Desperation produces poor terms. Poor terms reduce profit. Reserves increase negotiation strength. Strength improves deal quality. Quality improves returns. Cash on hand increases courage. Courage increases action speed.

Debt is treated as a tool, not a lifestyle extension. Builders distinguish productive debt from consumptive debt. Productive debt funds assets that produce return. Consumptive debt funds depreciation and delay. Each debt decision is tested against return potential. Interest cost must be justified by income gain. Builders avoid debt that feeds image instead of output. Image does not repay principal. Assets can repay principal. Careful leverage supports acceleration. Careless leverage destroys stability. Discipline keeps debt constructive.

Tracking becomes a daily habit instead of a quarterly surprise. Builders review cash position, burn rate, and allocation flow frequently. Frequent review produces fast correction. Fast correction prevents drift. Simple dashboards outperform complex neglect. Numbers become navigational instruments. Instruments guide adjustment. Adjustment preserves direction. Direction preserves momentum. Momentum preserves growth. What is measured stays managed. What stays managed can scale.

Cash discipline ultimately reflects identity, not technique alone. You become someone who commands money instead of being commanded by it. Each dollar receives orders, not permission. Spending becomes strategic, not emotional. Saving becomes purposeful, not fearful. Investing becomes systematic, not impulsive. Control becomes normal behavior. Normal behavior produces predictable outcomes. Predictable outcomes enable confident expansion. Expansion produces seven-figure pathways. Builders are recognized by how they handle money before they have a lot of it. Discipline is the signature of those who scale.

10

MOMENTUM MACHINES: DAILY ACTIONS THAT COMPOUND INTO MILLIONS

Momentum machines are not bursts of heroic effort but structured daily actions that produce compounding progress. Most people underestimate how powerful small repeated wins become over time. They wait for big breakthroughs while ignoring daily build steps. Millionaire builders think differently about progress. They design routines that manufacture forward motion every day. Motion creates feedback, feedback creates adjustment, and adjustment creates acceleration. The goal is not occasional intensity but perpetual advancement. When progress becomes automatic, growth becomes predictable. Predictable growth becomes scalable wealth. Momentum is not luck; it is engineered repetition.

A momentum machine begins with clearly defined daily non-negotiables tied directly to revenue and value creation. These are not general productivity tasks but economic drivers. Each day includes actions that create leads, improve offers, or build assets. You identify the few actions that move money forward. Those actions receive protected time first. Completion matters more than comfort. Builders finish their non-negotiables before optional work begins. This creates daily forward traction. Traction builds confidence. Confidence fuels consistency. Consistency fuels compounding.

Compounding power comes from frequency multiplied by direction. Repeated action in the wrong direction compounds failure. Repeated action in the right direction compounds fortune. Momentum machines are aligned with measurable outcomes. Every daily action connects to a larger metric. You are not just busy; you are advancing. Alignment prevents wasted motion. Wasted motion drains motivation. Directed motion builds belief. Belief strengthens discipline. Discipline strengthens repetition. Repetition strengthens results.

Momentum machines reduce startup friction so action begins quickly each day. Preparation happens before performance hours begin. Tools are set, plans are written, and targets are visible. Decision fatigue is minimized through pre-planning. When work starts, execution starts immediately. Fast starts preserve energy. Preserved energy increases output. Output increases progress signals. Progress signals increase motivation. Motivation reinforces repetition. Reduced friction sustains flow.

Measurement turns daily action into a visible winning streak. Builders track completions, not intentions. Checkmarks are psychologically powerful. Visible streaks discourage breaks in discipline. Scoreboards make progress tangible. Tangible progress increases persistence. Persistence increases total output. Output increases opportunity. Opportunity increases revenue. Tracking transforms effort into evidence. Evidence sustains drive.

Momentum machines are built around lead indicators, not just lag results. Revenue is a lag indicator. Daily outreach, creation, and improvement are lead indicators. Builders focus on what they can control today. Control increases confidence. Confidence increases speed. Speed increases cycles of learning. Learning improves effectiveness. Effectiveness increases yield. Yield increases revenue. Lead actions predict future results. Daily drivers determine monthly outcomes.

Environment automation supports momentum by making right action easier than wrong action. Distractions are blocked during build hours. Workspaces are optimized for focus. Default behaviors favor creation. Creation beats consumption. Consumption is scheduled after production. Builders design surroundings that vote for progress. Progress-friendly environments reduce willpower strain. Reduced strain increases consistency. Consistency increases compounding. Environment becomes a silent partner in success.

Momentum machines include daily learning loops tied to application. Builders do not just work; they refine. Each day includes review and improvement. Small optimizations accumulate into major gains. Reflection turns experience into strategy. Strategy improves tomorrow's actions. Better actions produce better outcomes. Outcomes produce better data. Data produces better decisions. Decisions produce better direction. Improvement becomes continuous.

Recovery cycles are integrated so momentum does not collapse from burnout. Sustainable pace beats short sprints. Builders schedule rest strategically. Energy is managed like capital. Sleep, movement, and renewal protect performance. Protected performance preserves streaks. Preserved streaks maintain compounding. Compounding requires continuity. Continuity requires sustainability. Sustainability requires recovery. Rest is part of the machine.

Momentum machines ultimately transform identity from occasional performer to daily producer. You stop relying on mood and start relying on mechanism. Mechanism produces output whether emotions cooperate or not. Daily production becomes your normal state. Normal production creates abnormal results over time. Small daily wins stack into massive annual gains. Annual gains stack into seven-figure trajectories. The machine you build in your days builds the wealth in your future. You do not wait for momentum; you manufacture it. Millions are not made in moments but in managed daily motion.

11

SCALING WITHOUT CHAOS: GROWING REVENUE WITHOUT LOSING CONTROL

Scaling without chaos is the difference between a business that grows and a business that breaks. Many people chase revenue expansion without operational stability. They celebrate bigger numbers while ignoring bigger cracks. Millionaire builders understand that growth must be supported by structure. Revenue that outruns control creates stress, waste, and reputation damage. True scale is not just more sales; it is more sales handled smoothly. Smooth handling preserves customer trust and team performance. Trust and performance protect long-term value. Growth must be engineered, not improvised. Controlled expansion beats explosive disorder. Stability is a scaling strategy.

The first principle of scaling without chaos is process before volume. If a process fails at ten customers, it will collapse at one hundred. Builders fix the machine before increasing the load. They map workflows step by step. Each step is tested for clarity and repeatability. Bottlenecks are identified early. Early fixes are cheaper than late rescues. Rescue mode destroys margin and morale. Clean processes increase confidence in growth campaigns. Confidence supports bolder expansion. Order enables acceleration.

Documentation is the backbone of controlled scale. What lives only in your head cannot scale safely. Builders write operating procedures for all critical tasks. Procedures turn guesswork into guidance. Guidance reduces variation. Reduced variation increases quality consistency. Consistency builds brand trust. Trust increases repeat business. Repeat business stabilizes revenue. Written playbooks reduce training time. Faster training supports faster growth. Documentation is scale insurance.

Capacity planning prevents overload before it happens. Builders forecast demand against delivery ability. They measure how much work each system and person can handle. Expansion plans include capacity thresholds. Thresholds trigger hiring, automation, or process redesign. This prevents surprise breakdowns. Surprises create chaos. Predictability creates calm. Calm supports decision quality. Decision quality supports profitability. Planning protects pace.

Technology is used deliberately to stabilize scaling operations. Tools are chosen to reduce manual strain. Automation handles repetitive workflows. Integrated systems reduce duplication and error. Dashboards provide real-time visibility. Visibility enables fast correction. Fast correction prevents escalation. Software becomes structural support. Support reduces operational stress. Reduced stress improves performance. Smart tools anchor scale.

Financial control intensifies during scaling phases. Rapid growth can hide waste and leakage. Builders increase financial review frequency when revenue rises. Expense ratios are tracked closely. Unit economics are monitored weekly. Profitability per product or client is measured.

Measurement prevents growth illusions. Illusions cause reckless spending. Data-driven scaling preserves margin. Margin funds further expansion. Control protects cash.

Team structure evolves intentionally as scale increases. Role clarity replaces informal multitasking. Each function receives ownership. Ownership increases accountability. Accountability increases reliability. Reliability supports higher volume. Builders avoid vague shared responsibility. Clear roles reduce conflict and delay. Decision rights are defined. Defined authority speeds execution. Structured teams scale smoothly.

Communication rhythms are formalized to prevent scaling confusion. Informal updates fail under higher complexity. Builders install regular reporting cycles. Metrics are shared transparently. Issues surface earlier through structured check-ins. Early surfacing enables fast solutions. Fast solutions prevent cascade failures. Alignment meetings maintain direction. Direction reduces duplicated effort. Reduced duplication increases efficiency. Communication is a scaling tool.

Quality control systems protect reputation during rapid growth. Increased volume increases error risk. Builders install checkpoints and review stages. Reviews catch defects early. Early detection reduces customer impact. Customer impact affects brand trust. Trust affects lifetime value. Quality metrics are tracked continuously. Continuous tracking drives improvement. Improvement stabilizes delivery. Quality sustains scale.

Scaling without chaos ultimately depends on leadership discipline and design thinking. Builders grow on purpose, not impulse. They expand what works and repair what strains. They measure before multiplying. They strengthen foundations before adding floors. Controlled growth compounds value instead of stress. Systems carry the weight, not heroic effort. Predictable operations support bold targets. Order enables ambition. Discipline enables expansion. Millionaire-scale businesses are not just bigger; they are better organized.

12

FROM FIRST DOLLAR TO FIRST MILLION: THE REPEATABLE EXPANSION MODEL

From first dollar to first million is not a mystery journey but a repeatable expansion model built on deliberate stages. Most people think a million is reached through one breakthrough moment. Builders know it is reached through structured multiplication cycles. The first dollar proves possibility, but the first system proves repeatability. Repeatability is the real milestone. When you can produce a result once on purpose, you can produce it again with refinement. Refinement increases efficiency and margin. Margin increases reinvestment power. Reinvestment power increases scale speed. The path is not luck driven; it is loop driven. Expansion is engineered through repetition.

The first stage of the repeatable expansion model is proof of value. You must demonstrate that someone will pay for your solution. Not compliments, not interest, but payment. Payment is market truth. Truth replaces speculation. Builders chase proof before polish. Early transactions validate direction. Direction reduces wasted effort. Proof creates confidence. Confidence increases commitment.

Commitment increases output. Output increases opportunity.

Once proof exists, the second stage is controlled repetition. You deliver the same value again using the same core method. You resist the urge to constantly reinvent. Consistency reveals process gaps. Process gaps reveal improvement targets. Improvement increases reliability. Reliability increases customer satisfaction. Satisfaction increases referrals. Referrals reduce acquisition cost. Reduced cost increases margin. Margin increases reinvestment capacity. Repetition turns wins into workflows.

The third stage is process capture and standardization. You document how the result is produced. Documentation converts skill into system. Systems reduce variation in outcome. Reduced variation increases predictability. Predictability supports scaling decisions. Scaling decisions require confidence. Confidence comes from consistent delivery. Builders standardize before they multiply. Multiplying chaos multiplies damage. Multiplying order multiplies profit. Standardization is expansion fuel.

The fourth stage is volume through focused channels. Builders identify where buyers come from and concentrate effort there. They double down on working acquisition paths. Scattered marketing slows expansion. Focused marketing accelerates traction. Traction increases deal flow. Deal flow increases revenue stability. Stability supports hiring and tooling. Tools and talent increase capacity. Capacity supports higher volume. Focus creates force. Force drives growth.

The fifth stage is margin improvement before aggressive scaling. More revenue with weak margins creates fragile growth. Builders optimize pricing, delivery cost, and efficiency early. Each percentage of margin matters. Strong margins fund experimentation. Experimentation finds breakthroughs. Breakthroughs increase leverage. Leverage increases output per unit effort. Margin is growth oxygen. Oxygen sustains expansion. Profit quality matters as much as revenue size. Healthy margins protect the climb.

The sixth stage is reinvestment loops that compound capability. Builders cycle profits into growth drivers. They invest in marketing engines, automation, and assets. Each reinvestment increases production power. Production power increases revenue ceiling. Ceiling lifts enable new targets. Targets drive innovation. Innovation improves offers. Better offers convert faster. Faster conversion accelerates cash flow. Cash flow feeds reinvestment again. The loop strengthens with discipline.

The seventh stage is team and tool leverage integration. Expansion eventually exceeds solo capacity. Builders prepare delegation frameworks early. They bring in help with documented processes. Tools support team efficiency. Efficiency supports output quality. Quality supports reputation. Reputation supports premium pricing. Premium pricing increases margin. Margin increases reinvestment speed. Leverage multiplies throughput. Throughput multiplies revenue.

The eighth stage is expansion through duplication, not constant invention. Builders replicate winning models into adjacent markets or segments. They reuse proven frameworks. Reuse reduces risk. Reduced risk increases speed. Speed increases capture of opportunity windows. Opportunity capture increases revenue growth rate. You clone success patterns with smart adaptation. Adaptation preserves relevance. Relevance preserves conversion. Duplication is safer than perpetual novelty. Repeat wins scale faster.

From first dollar to first million is achieved when these stages operate as a continuous cycle, not a one-time path. Proof leads to repetition, repetition to systems, systems to scale, and scale to reinvestment. Each loop increases strength and speed. Builders monitor each stage with metrics. Metrics guide adjustment. Adjustment preserves direction. Direction preserves momentum. Momentum preserves growth. Growth compounds into seven figures over time. The model is repeatable because the behaviors are repeatable. Millionaire expansion is not magic; it is method.

AFTERWORD

You are no longer standing at the starting line wondering if seven figures is possible. You have seen the mechanics, the models, the disciplines, and the decisions that build it step by step. The difference now is not information — it is activation. Wealth is no longer a mystery to you; it is a method waiting on your movement. The path is not reserved for the lucky, the connected, or the fearless. It belongs to the consistent executor who refuses drift and chooses deliberate progress.

Seven figures is not built in a single leap but in thousands of kept promises to yourself. It is built in the days you allow structure to lead and excuses to lose. It is built when you launch before comfort, measure before emotion, and reinvest before indulgence. It grows when your skills stack, your offers strengthen, your systems multiply, and your discipline holds the line. Every revenue action you take is a vote for your future balance sheet. Every controlled decision is a brick in your financial architecture.

Do not wait for a perfect season, perfect confidence, or perfect clarity. Builders create clarity by building.

Momentum is not found — it is forged through daily forward motion. Your first dollar proved you can produce value. Your next dollars prove you can repeat it. Your systems prove you can scale it. Your discipline proves you can keep it.

Start now, refine fast, measure always, and expand deliberately. Let others debate and delay. You will build and iterate. Let others admire opportunity. You will extract and execute. The fast track is not a shortcut — it is a commitment to intelligent speed and controlled scale.

Your first million is not a dream anymore.

It is a construction project.

And construction starts today.

ALSO BY DESHAWN PRICE

Toxic Amnesia: When Survival Becomes Self-Destruction

Toxic Strength: When Survival Looks Strong but Feels Empty

Toxic Control: When Fear Disguises Itself as Safety

Toxic Validation: When Approval Replaces Identity

Toxic Loyalty: When Faithfulness Becomes Self-Betrayal

Toxic Forgiveness -: When Grace Is Given Without Boundaries

Toxic Hope: When Waiting Turns Into Wasting Away

The Monetized Viral Machine: How to Build Posts That Pay

The Story-Selling Blueprint: Influence Hearts, Not Just Feeds

Victory Protocol: Strategic Habits That Produce Daily Wins

Your First Million: The Practical Path from Broke to Breakthrough

www.ingramcontent.com/pod-product-compliance
Lightning Source LLC
LaVergne TN
LVHW090431210926
848480LV00002B/783
* 9 7 9 8 2 3 3 7 2 9 1 1 9 *